MW00770827

Produced by JaDon Management Inc.
1405 4th Ave. N. W. #109
Ardmore, Ok. 73401

ISBN: 978-1-937501-14-3

Cover Design by:
Jeffrey T. McCormack
Apologia Book Shoppe
www.apologiabooks.com

The New Covenant: Fulfilled or Future?

Don K. Preston (D. Div.)

An Examination of the Dispensational Claim that the Promised New Covenant of Jeremiah 31 Has Not Been Fulfilled.

Foreword

Dispensationalism is, without a doubt, the dominant view of eschatology in America today. It wields tremendous influence even in the political arena under the name of Zionism. I am convinced that Dispensationalism / Zionism is a huge detriment to the cause of Christ.

Now, let me make it perfectly clear that I fully realize that most of those who espouse Dispensationalism are honest, God loving people whose desire is to serve the Lord. They have no intention whatsoever to slander the name of Christ and bring dishonor on his name or His Word. They are wonderful, sincere believers. But, that does not change the fact that the system itself is flawed, badly flawed, and actually poses a threat to world peace.

I cannot develop that particular claim at this time and in this work. There are a myriad of scholarly works and good men that see the danger and are speaking and writing about it, so, I urge the reader to avail yourself of some of those resources.

The focus of this work is on the promise of Jeremiah 31:29-31 where the Lord promised to make a New Covenant with the whole house of Israel. The Dispensational world tells us, in work after work, that God's promises to Israel have nothing to do with the "Gentile church." The church does not receive the blessings promised to Israel. This sharp, and tragic, dichotomization between God's promises to Israel and the church has and does lead to a depreciation of the value, the glory and the destiny of the blood bought body of Christ, and that is truly tragic.

The New Testament writers were almost all Jews. They tell us that their soteriological and eschatological promises were nothing but the hope of Israel, the promises found in the Old Testament. This is stunningly, incredibly important, since Zionism claims that the NT writers were concerned about and with the church and not Israel. We are told that although Christ came to establish the Kingdom – and thus, the New Covenant - due to Jewish unbelief, he could not do it. Instead, the church, given to the Gentiles until the time of the rapture, was established. At the Second Coming of Christ, that Jeremiad Covenant will then be made with Israel - not the church.

However, the NT tells a totally different story. As just stated, the NT writers were all Jews, anticipating the fulfillment of God's Old Covenant promises made to Old Covenant Israel. And what is truly challenging to the Dispensational paradigm is that they tell us, over and over again, that those OT promises made to Israel were being, and would be, fulfilled in Christ and the church! In other words, the New Testament writers knew nothing of a postponed kingdom. They knew *nothing* of the failure of God's plans and promises. They knew *nothing* of a future plan and promise distinctive to Israel, divorced from the church!

This book addresses but one of those Old Covenant promises made to Israel. That was the promise of the New Covenant. Make no mistake, that promise was in fact given to "the house of Israel and the house of Judah." That cannot be denied, and should not be! But, the question is, how do the NT writers, fully aware of that Old Covenant promise interpret that promise?

To state the case ever so briefly, they believed that beginning on Pentecost, that promise was being literally fulfilled. God was keeping His promise to Israel! But, what happened on Pentecost, with literal Israel, was not what was expected.

The NT epistles quote from Old Covenant prophecy repeatedly, promises that Israel interpreted in a literalistic, nationalistic manner as the modern Dispensationalists do. But, the NT writers tell us that those promises were not promises of a literal restoration of national Israel, in a physical land and city. Rather, those promises are interpreted and applied, through the Spirit, to Israel's spiritual restoration under Messiah.

Thus, Paul could say that the remnant of Israel was in fact receiving what Israel longed for (Romans 11:7), while the corporate body rejected the message of fulfillment. But, if the remnant was receiving what was promised to Israel, and yet, the remnant was not being restored to the land, to the literal City, with a literal, rebuilt Temple, then there is something fundamentally wrong with modern Zionism!

The promise of the New Covenant in Jeremiah is one of the most critical of all the promises made to Israel. If the Dispensationalists are right, and that New Covenant has not been established, we must view the Gospel in a totally different light. In fact, we must view it as insufficient and temporary, in direct conflict with what the New Testament says about the Gospel.

It is my prayer that the reader of this work will not be offended in any way. It is not my purpose or desire to offend in any manner. I want simply to share the reality that God kept His promises to Israel. He established the New Covenant just as promised, and that New Covenant is the Gospel of Jesus Christ, purchased with His blood. It will never be replaced. It will never be annulled. It will never cease to function. It is in and through the *Gospel* - and the Gospel alone - not a different, inferior covenant to be made exclusively with Israel - that men can and do have life.

My prayer is that this work will help the reader to see the glory of Christ's New Covenant- the Gospel - and not hold to a false hope of another, different Covenant.

NT writers tell us OT promises (O Covenant Phophec) were not promises of a litual restoration of national Israel in physical lands + city. Rather, those promises are interpreted and applied (thorough the Spirit) to Israel's spiritual restoration under Messiah

I WILL MAKE A NEW COVENANT!
Don K. Preston D. Div.

God's promise to make a New Covenant with Israel (Jeremiah 31:29f), is one of the most important promises of the entire Old Covenant. Most Christians today would affirm that we are under a New Covenant. The sacrificial world of Israel has been removed and Christ's perfect sacrifice is our atonement. Yet, what is not normally advertised is that *the Dispensational world does not believe that Jeremiah's prophecy of the New Covenant, has been established.*

This may seem shocking to many readers, but believe me, it is the view held by the leaders in the Dispensational camp. In fact, just a few days before putting the final touches on this book, I heard a minister on a Dallas, Texas radio program say something like the following: "I know most people believe the New Covenant of Jeremiah 31 has been established and that they think it is the gospel. But, that is not the truth! The New Covenant of Jeremiah will not be established until the Lord comes again."

There are, in the millennial world, three differing views concerning the New Covenant of Jeremiah 31.

First, some progressive Dispensationalists argue that the New Covenant has been "partially fulfilled" in the church. This view is by and large strongly rejected by most classical Dispensationalists.

Second, there is what is known as the Two Covenant theory. This view suggests that there are two New Covenants, one for the church, the current gospel of grace, and the other (Jeremiah 31), for Israel exclusively, in the millennium. There is also the view of John Hagee that the Jews of today do not need to be evangelized, since they are still the direct heirs of the Abrahamic Covenant, and will be saved through that.

Third, the consensus view per Russell Penney, is that the church in no way fulfills the New Covenant promise of Jeremiah 31, but that the church is nonetheless, "somehow 'receiving the benefits' from the New

Covenant." I suggest that the claim that the church is somehow receiving the benefits of a *non-existent covenant* is the epitome of sophistry. How can anyone receive the benefits of something that does not exist? That is somewhat like saying, "I don't have a million dollars in the bank, but I receive the benefits of that (non-existent), million dollar account!"

The consensus among millennialists is that the New Covenant has not yet been established with Israel. If, however, it can be shown that the New Covenant has indeed been established, in the words of Penney, "there is no pre-tribulational rapture."[1]

Walvoord says that if it could be proven that the New Covenant has been established, "it would be a crushing blow to the premillennial contention that there is a future kingdom."[2]

Pentecost says that, "If the church is fulfilling Israel's promises as contained in the New Covenant or anywhere in the scriptures, then (Dispensational) Premillennialism is condemned."[3]

I need now to outline the millennial concept of the New Covenant for the reader to understand that paradigm a bit better.

1.) God promised to make the New Covenant with Judah and Israel, not with the church. Per Dispensationalism, the distinction between Israel and the church is one of the most critical and foundational tenets of Biblical theology. The church does not receive Israel's promises, and Israel does not receive the blessings of the church. Of course, it is

---

[1] Russell L. Penney, Tyndale Theological Seminary, Ft. Worth, Tx., "The Relationship of the Church to the New Covenant." Internet article at: www.conservativeonline.org/journals/02_07_journal/1998v2n7_id05.htm.

[2] John Walvoord, *Major Bible Prophecies*, (Grand Rapids, Zondervan, 1991)186.

[3] Dwight Pentecost, *Things To Come*, (Grand Rapids, Zondervan, 1957)116.

insisted that the blessings of forgiveness belong to both entities, but, in the Dispensational paradigm, Israel receives forgiveness through the Jeremiad Covenant, *which is not the gospel of Christ.*

2.) Due to Israel's rebellion and unbelief, the church has temporarily replaced Israel in God's program. Israel's kingdom program has been suspended and postponed until the rapture. Ice cites Gentry, who says that the church has superceded Old Israel for all time, and responds by saying: "I could almost agree with his definition if he removed the phrase 'all time.' We dispensationalists believe that the church has superseded Israel during the current church age, but God has a future time in which He will restore national Israel 'as the institution for the administration of divine blessings to the world.'"[4]

Needless to say, Ice's view, common among Dispensationalism, raises the specter of a "reverse Replacement Theology." If it is insulting to say that the blood bought body of Christ has replaced - as the fulfillment, not the failure - of God's promises to Israel, what is it to say that one day, God will replace that blood-bought body with the nation of Israel?

3.) At the rapture, the church will be removed from this world, and God will resume His kingdom program with Israel.

4.) Israel signs the peace treaty with the anti-Christ, and, "Judaism is revived, and traditional sacrifices and ceremonies are re-instituted in the rebuilt temple in Jerusalem."[5]

---

[4] *Pre-Trib Perspectives*, P. O. Box 14111, Arlington, Tx., Vol. VII, Number 3, August (2002).

[5] Thomas Ice and Timothy Demy, *Prophecy Watch*, (Eugene, Ore, Harvest House, 1998)60.

-3-

5.) The anti-Christ breaks the treaty with Israel, sets up the Abomination of Desolation and the Great Tribulation ensues. At its worst point, Jesus descends from heaven for the destruction of the forces of evil and the millennial reign ensues.

6.) With the salvation of Israel in the millennium, Jeremiah's promise of the New Covenant is finally realized.

7.) Under the Jeremiad Covenant, Jerusalem is fully restored. Jesus sits on the literal throne of David. The temple is rebuilt (again). The priesthood is restored. Animal sacrifices are re-instituted, *again*. Circumcision is once again mandated by God.

While an examination of each of these distinctives would take volumes, for our purposes here, I want to ask, *what happens to the gospel of Christ when this proposed Jeremiad Covenant is established and the temple cultus is restored?*

MILLENNIALISM AND THE GOSPEL OF CHRIST

All believers would - I think - agree that the gospel of Christ, sanctified by his blood, is a marvelous thing, almost beyond description! ☛Through and under the gospel we are saved by grace through faith, not by Law.

☛Through and under the gospel all men in Christ are one. There are not to be any ethnic, social, political, economic, or other barriers between us.

☛Through and under the gospel man is free from the restrictions of the Old Law and being judged in regard to meat, drink, new moons, feast days, and the observance of days, weeks, months and years (Galatians 4; Colossians 2).

☛Through and under the gospel the law of circumcision as a characteristic identifying mark of the child of God is removed, for we receive the circumcision of the heart, a circumcision not made with hands, in faith and baptism (Colossians 2:11-12).

☛Through and under the gospel all believers are priests unto God, to offer up spiritual sacrifices (Hebrews 13:15; Revelation 1:5f).

☛Through and under the gospel, because we have the forgiveness of sin, animal sacrifices have been abolished because, "where there is remission of sin, there is no more sacrifice for sin" (Hebrews 10:16-18).

☛Through and under the gospel, we memorialize the deliverance from sin and death through His sacrifice, in our Communion Supper. The Communion Supper is the memorial of deliverance. It is not "for atonement," but a celebration of atonement, and deliverance from death!

I do not know of any millennialists that would deny the general validity of these statements. So, why would I state these universally agreed upon doctrines, in our discussion of the promised Jeremiad New Covenant and the proposed millennium? Here is why.

Our millennial friends believe that when the Jeremiad New Covenant is established in the proposed millennium things are different.

1. In the millennium Jew and Gentile distinctions will be restored. Pentecost says, "Gentiles will be the servants of Israel during that age." (*1957*, 508). When the reign of Jehovah-Jesus is established, "the distinction of Israel from the Gentiles will again be resumed" (Pentecost, 1957, 519). He then cites Unger, who says that in the millennium, Israel is blessed directly, and the Gentiles only mediately and subordinately to the Jews--a state of things in diametrical contrast to Christianity." (1957, 527).

2. In the millennium those who do not observe the Sabbaths, the new moons, the feast days, the pilgrimages, etc. are condemned by JHVH This is based on Ezekiel 43-45 as well as Zechariah 14.

3. In the millennium, those not circumcised cannot enter Jerusalem to worship, and without this privilege, they are condemned. (The question of circumcision in the millennium is one that Dispensationalists do not, understandably, like to discuss. However, in countless private discussions, and in formal public debates, I have asked millennialists if circumcision will be required in the millennium, and the invariable answer has been "Yes." They have no recourse but to believe this based on Ezekiel 44:9).

4. In the millennium, the Levitical priesthood is restored, and the priesthood of all believers is abolished. This is another theme that is disturbing to the millennialists. They like to deny that the Levitical priesthood will be restored, insisting instead that it will be a *Zadokite* priesthood. This is obfuscation. The Zadokites were Levitical!

5. In the millennium, the animal sacrifices that have now been caused to cease and are forbidden due to the efficacious sacrifice of Christ, will be re-instituted and restored. In a radio debate with noted Dispensationalist J. Randall Price, I asked him if animal sacrifices

would be restored in the millennium, in light of the fact that Christ's sacrifice now abolishes them. He answered that while animal sacrifices are now abolished in Christ, that, "this does not mean that is the way it will be in the millennium." (Unfortunately, the archive of that debate was eliminated when the radio network that carried it sold, and they erased all previous programming).

6. In the millennium, the Supper that memorializes our deliverance from sin and death will be abolished, and the animal sacrifices "for atonement" will be restored (Ezekiel 44-45).

Dispensationalists are very divided on the issue of the purpose of sacrifices in the millennium. Scofield insisted that they were to be memorial (Bible foot note on Ezekiel 43). On the other hand, Ice and Demy insist that this is not accurate stating that the millennial sacrifices "are for atonement rather than memorial." (*Prophecy Watch*, 261). To admit that the restored bloody cult of Israel will be restored, for the purpose of "making the atonement" should be troubling to all serious students of the Bible. This is a rejection of the efficacy of Christ's work of Atonement. And of course, it raises the issue of the means of justification in the Millennium.

Justification is by grace, through faith, under the gospel of Christ (Ephesians 2:8-9). Salvation by faith in Christ "is" the gospel, the good news. But, clearly, the Jeremiad Covenant is not the gospel and the gospel is not the Jeremiad Covenant, or so we are told. So, what is the means by which salvation comes? The description and prescriptions of the Jeremiad Covenant do not provide salvation by grace through faith! Instead, as just suggested, animal sacrifices are "for atonement."

It must be remembered that all of these praxis will be *mandated* by the New Covenant promised by Jeremiah. So, if the Jeremiad New Covenant will command the observance of all of these practices *that are now forbidden by, or mandated by the gospel of Christ*, we have to ask our question again, *what happens to the gospel of Jesus when this proposed Jeremiad Covenant is established, and the temple cultus is restored in the proposed Dispensational view of the Millennium?*

Flaming Fire book

THE MILLENNIUM AND THE GOSPEL

We need to ask some more questions at this juncture:

Is the church on earth during the *millennium*? According to the millennialists it is, having returned with Christ at the *parousia*.[6]

If the church is on earth in the millennium, what happens to the gospel, Christ's covenant with the church? *What covenant will Christians be under?*

Will Christians be under the current covenant of grace that forbids physical circumcision, a genealogically based priesthood, a centralized literal temple, ethnic distinctions, and animal sacrifices? If Christians remain under the covenant of grace, forbidden to do those things, then what happens to them when they do not go to Jerusalem to worship? The millennialists say Zechariah 14, teaches that in the millennium all men must pilgrimage to Jerusalem or be cursed and condemned. What about the Christian who knows that "neither in this mountain or in Jerusalem will men worship the Father," is his mandate (John 4:20-24)? If, at this juncture, the millennialists says, "Well, that is the way things are *now*, but that is not how it will be *then*," *that is our entire point*! What happens to the gospel that nullifies geo-centric worship? Is the gospel nullification of geo-centric worship nullified and abrogated?

---

[6] There is a huge, but seldom addressed issue for the Dispensationalist in regard to the church, the rapture and the Great Tribulation. Ice and other pre-tribulation rapture advocates are adamant that the church is not on earth during the Great Tribulation, or, at the Second Coming of Christ, that occurs seven years after the rapture. The insurmountable problem is that virtually all of these men say that 2 Thessalonians speaks of the Second Coming. Well, that text promised the church– not Israel– relief from persecution "when the Lord Jesus is revealed from heaven." The Lord could hardly give the church relief from persecution at his parousia, if the church is not on earth, under persecution, at his coming! See my development of this in my *In Flaming Fire* book, available on Amazon, Kindle, my websites and other retailers.

-8-

If the church is on earth during the millennium, what happens to the covenant of grace if a Christian refuses to be circumcised? Paul said, "in Christ neither circumcision nor uncircumcision avails anything, but the new creation" (Galatians 6:15), or, "I say to those of you who are circumcised that you are a debtor to keep the whole law" (Galatians 5:1-4), "those of you who seek to be justified by the Law (via circumcision, DKP), you are fallen from grace." Yet, according to the millennial tenets, no one that is uncircumcised can approach the Lord (Ezekiel 44:9). Further, no one can enter the city, nor worship at the Temple if uncircumcised (Isaiah 52.1). So, is the Christian under the covenant of grace that forbids circumcision, or under the Jeremiad Covenant that will ostensibly demand circumcision?

A brief word here about circumcision. W. D. Davies is certainly correct to note:

"To the unsympathetic mind, the observance of the Law, centering in the minutea of dietary laws and table-fellowship, could not but appear, at worst, antiquated superstition, and, at best, annoying, and anti-social priggishness: circumcision to such a mind could only suggest a barbaric survival. But often in history, as for example, the Puritan controversy over vestments, great issues have been fought in terms of trivia. So in the early church, battles for principles often centered around apparent piccadilloes. Throughout his treatment of circumcision and the Law, remote and pettifogging as they may seem, Paul was concerned with a central question: the nature and constitution of the people of God–its continuity and discontinuity with the Jewish people of history."[7]

The issue of circumcision, as Davies suggests, is of *foundational importance*. Circumcision was inextricably linked with possession of the Land, identity as the people of God, Temple privileges, (Cf. Acts 21), and much more. Thus, for Paul to say, repeatedly, that circumcision

---

[7] W. D. Davies, *The Gospel and the Land,* (Berkeley, University of California Press, 1974)171.

was of no value was one of the most theologically loaded, challenging, and even traumatic doctrines he could enunciate!

In my first public debate in 1983, I used the issue of circumcision as the basis of much of my argumentation. My Dispensational opponent was totally unprepared to deal with the issue, and I have not found a Dispensationalist that is. The nullification of circumcision effectively says that God's promises to *Abraham and to Israel* were fulfilled, and all of the physical, external markers of her as a distinctive covenant people were now removed through that fulfillment in Christ. Interestingly, not many authors deal with circumcision and its profound implications for Dispensationalism, and this is a bit perplexing.

Since the church is on earth in the millennium, and since the distinctions between Jews and Gentiles will once again be restored, as Pentecost and others insist, then does that mean that Peter's words to Cornelius, "you know how unlawful it is for a Jewish man to keep company with or go to one of another nation, " will once again be true, and religiously imposed (Acts 10:28)? When Peter met and ate with Gentiles, but then withdrew from the Gentiles upon the arrival of some of his faithful Jewish brethren, *Paul condemned him for his hypocrisy* (Galatians 2). But, which practice will be approved and mandated in the millennium? If the Jew/Gentile distinctions are restored, does that not mean that Peter was simply "ahead of his time" in his discriminatory actions?

As you can see, there is a real dilemma here. The Dispensational insistence that, "That is the way things are *now*, but not the way things will be in the millennium," in regard to Christian praxis, is one of the most overlooked or ignored issues in the entire controversy with Dispensationalism. This is a *huge problem*, because it even involves the obedience of saving faith and the differences between now and then in the millennial view. Pentecost says, "The expression of that saving faith will differ from the expressions that are required in the present day, but the sacrifices must be viewed as mere expressions of faith, and not the means of salvation." (*Things To Come*, 531). So there you have it, even the very expressions of saving faith that are mandated by the gospel are totally different from how things will be in the millennium!

-10-

God's Word will be fundamentally, radically altered, distorted, and modified, as to be unrecognizable.

What I want to do now is to illustrate just a few of the radical changes that will, of necessity if the Dispensational paradigm is true, take place in the fundamental nature of the gospel of Christ. I offer these things, certainly not to offend my Dispensational friends, but, to hopefully open the eyes of everyone to the radical nature of the New Covenant doctrine as espoused in the Dispensational world. With this in mind, let me give several examples of the current situation in Christ, under the gospel, in contrast to what our Dispensational friends say will take place under the future Jeremiad Covenant, in the Millennium.

✝ *Now*, in Christ, under the gospel, there is no geo-centric pilgrimage worship, but *then*, in the millennium, geo-centric, pilgrimage worship will be restored.

✝ *Now*, in Christ, under the gospel, there is no Temple worship mandated, for the church is the Temple of God, but *then*, in the millennium, under the Jeremiad Covenant, Temple worship will not only be restored but, refusal or failure to travel to Jerusalem to worship there will result in condemnation!

✝ *Now*, in Christ, under the gospel, there is no genealogically based priesthood, with exclusive rights to offer liturgical sacrifices, but *then*, in the millennium, under the Jeremiad Covenant, the Levitical, exclusionary, genealogically based priesthood will be restored.

✝ *Now*, in Christ, under the gospel, there is no animal sacrifice, since Christ's blood has brought remission of sin, but, *then*, in the millennium, under the Jeremiad Covenant, animal sacrifices will be offered "for atonement."

✝ *Now*, in Christ, under the gospel, there is no mandate to observe new moons, feast days, and Sabbaths, but *then*, in the Millennium, under the Jeremiad Covenant, all men will be required to observe the feast days, new moons and Sabbaths.

✝ *Now*, in Christ, under the gospel, there is no Jew and Gentile distinction, but *then*, in the millennium, under the Jeremiad Covenant, Jew and Gentile distinctions will be restored.

✝ *Now*, in Christ, under the gospel, there is no theologically mandated practice of physical circumcision, but *then*, in the millennium, under the Jeremiad Covenant, physical circumcision will once again be mandated by God.

As you can see, according to the millennial view of things, the Jeremiad Covenant will supposedly *restore virtually everything that the gospel now forbids*, and will *forbid much of what the gospel mandates*. Is it possible to so fundamentally alter, distort and pervert the gospel of Christ without completely *nullifying* it? And if you nullify the gospel, what then of the salvation brought by the gospel?

In light of these dilemmas, we might ask, are two covenants in existence during the millennium? Will the gospel continue to be the law for Christians, while the Jews are under the Jeremiad New Covenant?[8]

To understand the millennial view of these things, I emailed Thomas Ice, one of the leading proponents of Dispensationalism today, and with whom I have engaged in several debates.[9] I wanted to have direct input

---

[8] Those familiar with John Hagee know that he advocates a Two Covenant theology. He says that Jews do not need to convert to Christ, because they have their own, separate Covenant! This is a horrible, and tragic perversion of Truth!

[9] It is telling that Ice will not meet me in formal debate again, even though he has been challenged numerous times to do so. You can purchase a copy of my Florida debate with him from my websites.

from a contemporary, representative Millennialist. I asked Mr. Ice four questions concerning the New Covenant. I am including that correspondence here.

I am giving Ice's answers in their entirety, cut and pasted from his post, to avoid Ice's oft repeated charge that I misrepresent his positions. While he makes that charge, he has never documented a single instance of that being true.

In our public debate in Florida, October, 2003, Ice, during one of the breaks, charged me with misrepresenting his position. During the rest of the debate, when I quoted anything from Ice's writings, I said, "This is what is found in Thomas' writings. If he does not agree with the position I am citing from his books, he can please tell us what he really does believe." *He did not offer to correct a single one of my citations.* I should also note that Thomas Ice stated after that Florida debate, that will never debate me again.

During an earlier radio debate, I quoted directly from one of his books, (*Prophecy Watch*), in regard to Acts 2 and Joel 2. He vehemently denied that the quote was in the book, or that he believed what I was quoting, maintaining that I was misrepresenting him. I denied the charge and offered to verify the quote to him or to anyone else. The next day, Ice emailed me, asking for documentation for the quote. I immediately sent him the page number. He finally responded that the quote was in fact in the book, *but that he did not believe what was written*! He said the quote was from the co-author of the book (Timothy Demy), but that he, Ice, did not believe in the position stated by Demy. The fact is, I had not misrepresented the position stated in the book, nor would I ever knowingly misrepresent Ice's position, or anyone else's.

With this in mind, here are the questions that I posed to Ice, with his responses:

1. Do you believe that the New Covenant promised in Jeremiah 31/Ezekiel 37 has been established, in any sense at all?

Thomas Ice's answer: "I believe that the New Covenant is **applied** to the church today because of the clear statements of Luke 22:20, 1

Corinthians 11:25, and 2 Corinthians 3:6. The New Covenant in Jeremiah 31:31 will be made with 'the house of Israel and with the house of Judah.' Thus, it is not being **fulfilled** today, but will be in the millennium for Israel. Ezekiel 37:22 refers to the 'house of Israel.' I believe there are many other references that anticipate Israel's New Covenant found throughout the Old Testament (Deut. 29:4; 30:6; Isa. 59:20–21; 61:8–9; Jer. 32:37–40; 50:4–5; Ezek. 16:60–63; 34:25–26; 36:22–32; 37:21–28; Zech. 12:10)." (My emphasis, DKP. As noted above, exactly how it is that the church can have the blessings of a non existent covenant applied to it, is not explained by Ice or any other Dispensationalist. It is simply asserted. This is disingenuous at best).

2. If the New Covenant of Jeremiah 31/Ezekiel 37 has been established, is the church, the body of Christ, now living under that Covenant, subject to its mandates, and recipients of its blessings?
Thomas Ice's answer: "I do not believe that the New Covenant of Jeremiah 31 and Ezekiel 37 has been established yet."

3. In the proposed millennium, will there be only one covenant in effect, for all men?
Thomas Ice's answer: "I am only aware of a single covenant for the millennium."

4. Will there be two covenants in effect, applicable to different groups of people?
Thomas Ice's answer: "I do not think so since I only find the New Covenant being referenced in Scripture."

5. More specifically, in the proposed millennium, will the church be living under and subject to the gospel, while the Jews live under and are subject to the New Covenant of Jeremiah/Ezekiel?
Thomas Ice's answer: "Since the church began on the Day of Pentecost (Acts 2) and ends at the rapture, all members of the church (Jew and Gentiles) will be resurrected and reigning at the right hand of Christ as His Bride during the millennium. Since I am not sure of the

implications of your statement 'living under and subject to the gospel,' I cannot answer that. As I am sure you know, saved Jews and Gentiles who survived the tribulation will enter the millennium in their mortal bodies, having become believers after the rapture. Thus, the millennial rule of Christ will involve Jews and Gentiles under the rule of Christ with His Bride (the Church) reigning and ruling at His right hand (Rev. 3:21)." (Email exchange 3-7-05).

Allow me to express this simply:
There will only be one covenant in effect in the millennium. (The church, and all Jews and Gentiles will be subject to that one covenant in the millennium- Thomas Ice).

That one covenant will be the New Covenant promised in Ezekiel 37 and Jeremiah 31.

Therefore, the church and all Jews and Gentiles, will be subject to the covenant of Ezekiel 37 / Jeremiah 31 in the millennium.

In light of these answers, and Ice is certainly representative of other millennialists in his answers, we have to ask, again, *What happens to the gospel –the covenant of grace– in the millennium?* The answer can only be that it is the victim of *Reverse Replacement Theology*. While the gospel has temporarily replaced Israel, the gospel itself is doomed to be *permanently* replaced by the Jeremiad New Covenant! The gospel is replaced by the revised, revamped, re-instituted Old (New) Covenant.
We must note here that millennialists are adamant that the millennial Covenant is not the restoration of the *Mosaic Covenant*. They insist that the Mosaic Covenant has been forever "fulfilled and discontinued." (Ice, *Watch*, 258). However, it is maintained that the Jeremiad Covenant will be a mixture of Mosaic Covenant elements, and new elements added. Of course, this invites the reader to ponder that Jesus emphatically said you do not put new wine into old skins. This is self destructive (Mark 2.22). Pentecost admits the Mosaic system and the millennial system are "strangely alike" (*Things to Come*, 519). Indeed,

-15-

with a restored Land, Restored Jerusalem, Restored Temple, Restored Levitical priesthood, Restored altar, Restored sacrifices, Restored Feast days, etc, *all virtually identical to the Mosaic institutes*, one is hard pressed to justify saying that the millennial worship is not in fact the restoration of the Mosaic Covenant.

There is no way that one can claim that the practices proposed by the Dispensational view of the millennial Jeremiad Covenant will or could be, in any way whatsoever, the gospel of Jesus Christ. The millennial practices proposed by the Dispensational construct are, in the words of Unger cited by Pentecost earlier, "a state of things in diametrical contrast to Christianity."

I must confess my personal shock and revulsion of the very idea that any Christian would espouse and promote the replacement of the blood bought gospel of Christ and the church, "with a state of things in diametrical contrast to Christianity." Is this not an "anti-Christian" message? Does this not impugn Christ's work? I am convinced by many years of dialogue with Dispensationalists, that the average person "in the pews" is not aware of what is being taught by the leading proponents of Dispensationalism, and would in fact recoil in horror upon realizing that Dispensationalism advocates the removal of Christianity and its replacement with "a state of things in diametrical contrast to Christianity."

Unger is right. Yet, the proposed millennial practices are not only "in diametrical contrast to Christianity," they are in fact *condemned by the gospel of Christ!* So, if the things that the millennialists say will be mandated by the Jeremiad New Covenant are in fact God's will during the millennium, that *of necessity* demands that the gospel of Christ must be either suspended, altered, rejected, or nullified. You cannot posit the establishment of a New Covenant that will condemn or command the very things that the gospel condemns or commands without thereby demanding the suspension or abrogation of the gospel.

In the first century transitional period, the Old Covenant was "nigh unto passing away" (Hebrews 8:13), while the New Covenant was being revealed. The clash between the two covenant worlds is found on virtually every page of the New Testament. So, if there was a conflict between the two covenant worlds in the first century, as one covenant passed and another was instituted, how much more would this be the case if the gospel and the proposed Jeremiad Covenant were to exist side by side? In the first century, one covenant had to pass because it was inferior, because it was old, etc. Which covenant would / will have to give way in the millennium? Which covenant is better?

Paul said that circumcision was nullified by Christ's gospel, and that to practice it as a command of God nullifies grace and his gospel. How would that not be true in the millennium? The re-establishment of circumcision would be "a diametrical contrast to Christianity."

Paul taught that the practice of Jew and Gentile distinctions is a violation of the oneness for which Christ died. If the Jew and Gentile distinctions are restored, how does this not impugn the gospel for which Christ died? The restoration of ethnic distinctions would be "a diametrical contrast to Christianity."

Paul taught that because of the remission of sin through Christ's blood, animal sacrifices are abolished. If therefore animal sacrifices are restored "for an atonement," just exactly how does this not demand a rejection of Christ's sacrifice? The restoration of animal sacrifices would be "a diametrical contrast to Christianity."

Paul said that he was "afraid" of the Galatians (4:8f, and Colossians), for allowing themselves to be judged on whether they observed feast days, new moons, Sabbaths and eating restrictions. If those observances are mandated by the Jeremiad New Covenant, what happens to Paul's command not to be judged by those things? In fact, per the Dispensational view, in the millennium, failure to honor the Sabbath as well as the cultic feast days will result in condemnation! Needless to say, the restoration of the imposition of cultic feast days would be "a diametrical contrast to Christianity."

What happens to the gospel if the things it now condemns are mandated, and the things it now mandates are forbidden? What happens if the current "expressions of saving faith" are radically altered and transformed into a return to the practices now forbidden by the gospel? That would be "a diametrical contrast to Christianity." Is it possible to establish a system that is "a diametrical contrast to Christianity," without that system being *in opposition to the gospel?* Is it not "anti-gospel" to propose the replacement of the gospel with a system that is "a diametrical contrast to Christianity."

The Gospel is not the promised New Covenant of Jeremiah 31 says the Dispensationalist.

The Covenant of Jeremiah – to be established in the Millennial Reign, we are told - will mandate that everyone be circumcised, offer animal sacrifices, honor Jew / Gentile distinctions, honor the Sabbath and the Jewish feast days.

Failure to do those things results in condemnation and destruction- we are told.

But, the Gospel of Christ forbids observance of those things as a Christian duty.

So, what happens to the Gospel in the Millennium?
Will it - the unending Gospel - be annulled?

Will there be two covenants, for two people, and each of those two covenants condemning what the other commands?

This is hugely problematic- and the Dispensationalists have no answer for it!

---

the Dispensational problem

These are serious issues indeed! The only possible way to resolve this conundrum would be for one of two, or both, things to be true.

1. The proposed Jeremiad Covenant would have to be intrinsically *better* than the current gospel. Would any Millennialist wish to affirm that the proposed Jeremiad Covenant is intrinsically *better than the gospel?* Go back and read carefully about the blessings that the Gospel provides us, and ask what could be better?

2. It would have to be shown that the gospel, due to the coming of the better Jeremiad Covenant, was *predicted to be replaced.* As we will see

below, even the millennialists admit that the gospel is better than the old cultic practices, and further, *they admit that the gospel of Christ will never pass away or become inoperative!*

It will not do to say that Paul was contrasting the Mosaic cultic practices with the gospel, but that it is different in the millennium, because the Jeremiad New Covenant is not a restoration of the Mosaic covenant. *That is totally irrelevant!*

We must emphasize here that Paul condemned circumcision, as noted above. Circumcision was not a strictly Mosaic Covenant practice. It was *Abrahamic*! Thus, Paul's rejection of circumcision is a total refutation of the idea that the Mosaic Covenant has been forever removed, but that the Abrahamic Covenant has not been fulfilled. Nothing was more central to the Abrahamic Covenant than circumcision, and Paul unequivocally said that circumcision had lost its theological significance because of the faithfulness of God in keeping His promises.

The fact is that the Jeremiad Covenant practices proposed by the millennialists are, in essence, the very things that are diametrically opposed to the gospel. Does it matter whether it was the *Mosaic* Jew and Gentile distinctions, or that it would be the *Jeremiad* Covenant Jew and Gentile distinctions? All such ethnic distinctions and discriminations are forbidden and condemned by the gospel!

It does not matter whether it was animal sacrifices mandated under the Pentateuch, or whether it would be animal sacrifices mandated by the Jeremiad Covenant. It did not matter whether it was Abel, Abraham, or *whoever*, offering animal sacrifices. Abraham's animal sacrifices were no better than those offered by and under Moses. The fact remains that God *never* desired the blood of bulls and goats (Hebrews 10:5f), and the very thought of offering bloody animal sacrifices "for atonement," is tantamount to a rejection of the atonement of Christ.

So, the proposed millennial Jeremiad Covenant is nothing less than a rejection of the gospel of Christ. No amount of rationalization can justify the restoration of the things condemned by the gospel, or the rejection of those things mandated by the gospel. Does this not then *demand*, if the Jeremiad Covenant does restore these things, that the gospel will in fact be abolished? According to the millennialists this cannot be.

Unless it can be proven that the Jeremiad New Covenant will be superior to the Gospel of Christ,
or,
Unless it can be shown that the Gospel is to be annulled at the arrival of the Jeremiad New Covenant,
then,
It cannot be argued that there is a need for another New Covenant.
The gospel is for all men, Jew and Greek, not just one ethnic minority group!
No proposed Jeremiad New Covenant could ever improve on the gospel of Christ!

THE EVERLASTING GOSPEL OF JESUS CHRIST

The idea that the gospel of Christ, the gospel established by His blood, will be replaced, is directly counter to express statements of Scripture, and frankly, a horrid idea. Interestingly, *Dispensationalists actually agree that the gospel will never be annulled, or removed*. In an article attempting (unsuccessfully), to refute some of my writings and statements, Thomas Ice appealed to Matthew 24.35. His topic was the "heaven and earth," and he was attempting to show that the term is not used metaphorically.

Ice's contention that the term "heaven and earth" is not used metaphorically falls to the ground in Matthew 5.17f. Jesus said "until heaven and earth pass away, not one jot or one tittle shall pass from the Law, until it is all fulfilled." The topic here is the Mosaic Covenant. Jesus said "heaven and earth" would not pass until the entirety of that Mosaic Torah was fulfilled. Thomas Ice believes that the Mosaic Torah has indeed passed away (*Prophecy Watch*, 258). If therefore, the Mosaic Law has passed away, then the "heaven and earth" of Matthew 5 has passed away. The dilemma here is acute for Dr. Ice. If he admits that the "heaven and earth" term is used metaphorically here, then his contention that the term is never so used falls to the ground. On the other hand, if he maintains his denial that the term is used metaphorically, then that means that until literal "heaven and earth" passes away, then the Mosaic Torah remains valid. This would demand that the Mosaic Law remains valid today. Ice cannot have it both ways.

I have, and do argue that in Matthew 24.35 Jesus was referring to the Old Covenant Temple as heaven and earth,[10] Ice argues: "This passage

---

[10] Josephus, first century Jewish historian, says the Jews described the Temple as "heaven and earth": "However, this proportion of the measures of the tabernacle proved to be an imitation of the system of the world: for the third part thereof which was within the four pillars, to which the priests were not admitted, is, as it were, a Heaven peculiar to God; but the space of the twenty cubits, is, as it were, sea and land, on

-21-

clearly states that, 'heaven and earth *will* pass away' one day, but in contrast to that Christ's words 'shall not pass away.' In order to strengthen the emphasis upon the absolute impossibility of His words passing away, Christ uses not one, but two Greek words that mean 'not,' (grouped together), to say that something will not happen. 'The double negative *ou me* with the subjunctive is the usual form for the emphatic negation,' notes Randolph Yeager.[11] Lenski agrees and says that *ou me* is used 'all-inclusively' and calls it 'the strongest negation.' Arnold Fruchtenbaum, often cited by Ice and LaHaye, says, "The law of Christ will never be rendered inoperable."[12]

All I can say to this is, Amen!

As Ice insists, Jesus was emphatically telling his disciples that his word will never pass away. The New Covenant of the Gospel of Christ will never cease to be operative. It will always be authoritative! That could not be clearer, and *that is precisely what I affirm*. However, *what is the word of Christ?* Is it not the gospel of Grace? Can anyone, *would anyone,* deny that? You simply must catch the power of this reality!

Follow closely.
✦ The word of Jesus Christ will never pass away (Matthew 24.35, Ice concurs).

✦ The word of Christ *is the current gospel, the covenant of grace.*

---

which men live, and so this is peculiar to the priests only..." Whiston, Josephus Antiquities, Bk. 3, chapter 6:4, (87).

[11] Randolph O. Yeager, *The Renaissance New Testament*, 18 vols. (Bowling Green, KY: Renaissance Press, 1978), vol. 3) 322.

[12] Arnold Fruchtenbaum, CTS Journal, vol. 5, #4, (1999)6.

✦ Therefore, the gospel of Jesus Christ–the current covenant of grace *will never pass away*! It will always be operative!

What that means should be obvious:

The current gospel of Christ will never pass away. There will never be a time when its commands and mandates are not authoritative.

But the current gospel of Christ forbids animal sacrifices, localized Temple worship, observance of feast days and the Sabbath, physical circumcision, etc..

Therefore, the current gospel of Christ, *since it will never pass away*, will never cease to forbid animal sacrifices, localized Temple worship, observance of the Sabbath and the feast days, physical circumcision, etc..

To use the words of Fruchtenbaum:

The gospel of Jesus Christ will never be rendered inoperative.

But the gospel of Christ forbids animal sacrifices, localized Temple worship, observance of the Sabbath and the feast days, physical circumcision, etc..

Therefore, the prohibition of animal sacrifices, localized Temple worship, observance of feast days, physical circumcision, etc. *will never be rendered inoperative*.

What Ice needed for Jesus to say was, "My word–The covenant of grace--will stand until it is taken out of the way - raptured with the church - so that Jeremiah's new millennial covenant is established." Of course, Ice cannot produce any passage that even remotely suggests that the gospel of Christ will ever be removed, abrogated, superceded, or mitigated in any way. The current kingdom of Christ cannot be moved

(Hebrews 12.28), and the Church age is the "age without end" (Ephesians 3.20f).

So, according to the view of Premillennial Dispensationalism, the gospel will never be rendered inoperable. Yet, the gospel forbids and condemns virtually every aspect of the proposed Jeremiad Covenant so foundational to the millennial view.

If the Jeremiad Covenant *commands* animal sacrifices, localized Temple worship, observance of the Sabbath and the feast days, physical circumcision, etc., but the gospel *forbids* animal sacrifices, localized Temple worship, observance of the Sabbath and the feast days, physical circumcision, etc., what shall inhabitants of the millennium do? *Which covenant do they obey?*

Remember that Ice says there will only be *one covenant* in force in the millennium, and that is the Jeremiad Covenant. The question then *demands* to be answered, what happens to the *unendingly operative gospel* that stands in *total opposition to the Jeremiad Covenant?*

Remember that Ice says that the church and Gentiles and Jews are all on earth together under Christ, *subject to only one covenant*, the covenant that Unger says is, "a state of things in diametrical contrast to Christianity." But how can the church, that is currently subject to the *unendingly operative gospel* that forbids ethnic distinctions, animal sacrifices, Sabbath observance, physical circumcision, temple worship, etc. *ever* be in subjection to a covenant that is "a state of things in diametrical contrast to Christianity?" Yet, the Dispensationalists insist that the Jeremiad Covenant– *not the gospel-- is the one and only covenant that will be in effect in the millennium, and that all men, including the church, will be subject to that covenant that stands in diametrical contrast to Christianity!*

There is no way to over-emphasize the inescapable dilemma of the Dispensational paradigm in regard to the New Covenant.

☛ They cannot argue that the gospel will be removed or altered, without denying the emphatic declarations of the Bible, not to mention their own declarations that *the gospel will never become inoperative.*

☛ They cannot argue that there will be two covenants in existence in the millennium, without violating their own writings that there will only be one covenant in the millennium, the Jeremiad Covenant.

☛ They cannot argue that the gospel will still be present but not *observed*, for that nullifies the gospel.

☛ They cannot argue that the gospel is the covenant of the millennium. The gospel forbids the fundamentals of the millennium as posited by the Dispensationalists.

The only way for the Millennialist to argue for the establishment of the Jeremiad Covenant, as the law of God for all people in the millennium, is nullify, abrogate or suspend the gospel of Jesus Christ– the true New Covenant.

As suggested above, I believe that the Dispensational world teaches the worst sort of Replacement Theology. Let's look closer at this issue.

The New Covenant and Replacement Theology

Our Dispensational Premillennial friends often castigate non-millennialists for preaching "replacement theology." Perhaps it is time for our friends to consider the consequences of their own doctrine.

Dispensationalism would *replace the blood bought covenant of grace with the Jeremiad Covenant* that cannot be the covenant Jesus died to establish, for *he died to establish the gospel and the church* (Acts 20:28). But the gospel and the church stand diametrically opposed to the things that our millennial friends say will exist in the millennium under the Jeremiad Covenant. Remember what Thomas Ice said in response to Kenneth Gentry.

Ice cites Gentry, who says the church has superceded Old Israel for all time, and responds by saying: "I could almost agree with his definition if he removed the phrase 'all time.' We dispensationalists believe that the church has superseded Israel during the current church age, but God has a future time in which He will restore national Israel 'as the institution for the administration of divine blessings to the world.'"[13] So, Thomas Ice affirms that the church has temporarily replaced Israel, but, in the proposed Millennium, Israel will replace the church "as the institution for the administration of divine blessings to the world."

This means it is not the church through whom the nations will be blessed– in spite of the fact that it is strictly those who are of faith - i.e. the body of Christ– that are the true seed of Abraham (Galatians 3:6f) - and thus, not only the recipients of the Abrahamic blessings, but the conduit of those blessings to the world.

This means that although Paul said that it in and through the body of Christ praise, honor and glory– not to mention the wisdom of God– would be manifested to the world forever, "age without end" (Ephesians 3:20f), that this state of affairs will be replaced. It is through Israel that

---

[13] *Pre-Trib Perspectives*, P. O. Box 14111, Arlington, Tx., Vol. VII, Number 3, August (2002).

Wow!

these blessings will then flow!

This means it is not the church that Christ died to establish, and which is the object of his salvation work (Ephesians 5:22f) that is the focus of his future work of blessing the world, but, the (supposedly) ethnic people for whom animal sacrifices were the means of "sanctification."

!! - Did Jesus die to establish two covenants, *one that condemns the other*? Did Jesus die to establish both the gospel and the Jeremiad Covenant, the gospel that condemns animal sacrifices, circumcision and discrimination, but then, in addition, the Jeremiad Covenant that will restore those things?

!! - Dispensationalism would *replace* the spiritual temple as the body of Christ, with a physical edifice.

!! - Dispensationalism would *replace* the spiritual priesthood of all believers, with the Zadokite priesthood.

!! - Dispensationalists - who, by and large are not Sabbatarian! - would replace the Sabbath rest of salvation that we now have in Christ, with the literal, seventy day Sabbath observance. Failure to keep the Sabbath will supposedly result in condemnation!

!! - Dispensationalism would *replace* equality in Christ, with the Jew / Gentile discriminatory practices.

!! - Dispensationalism would *replace* the spiritual circumcision of the heart, with physical circumcision.

!! - Dispensationalism would *replace* the atonement of Christ with the offering of bulls and goats for atonement.[14]

In light of all of these things, I think it is time to ask, who is it that teaches a dangerous *replacement theology*?

The final word on the New Covenant is that Christ's gospel gives today *every thing* that the promised Jeremiad Covenant promised. The gospel is everlasting (cf. Isaiah 55:3).[15] It is the covenant of peace (Ezekiel 37: 26). Through the blood of Christ, those who enter that New Covenant have the forgiveness of sins. No future covenant could give anything better, and *the New Covenant proposed by the millennial construct is not a better covenant*, based on better promises, with a better hope, than the gospel, nor could it ever be.

We began this work by asking, *what happens to the gospel of Christ when the proposed Jeremiad Covenant is established and the temple cultus is restored?* We have shown that in the millennial paradigm it is fundamentally essential *that the gospel of Christ be nullified*, and replaced by a system that is, "a state of things in diametrical contrast to Christianity." And yet, according to scripture, and even the Millennialist's own words, *there will never be a time when the gospel is inoperative*.

Since the gospel gives what the promised Jeremiad Covenant was to give, we conclude that the gospel of Christ is the promised Jeremiad

---

[14] I realize that Dispensationalists will cry "Foul" to this charge, but, the language of Ezekiel - taken literally as Dispensationalists insist that we do - is too clear. The animal sacrifices are clearly stated to be "to make atonement."

[15] Note that in Isaiah 55 God would make the everlasting covenant when he gave Israel's Messiah the "sure mercies of David." In Acts 13:34f, Paul stated emphatically-- *citing Isaiah*-- that God had given Christ the "sure mercies of David." This is inspired testimony that the New Covenant promises to Israel were even then being fulfilled.

Covenant. Further, since the gospel can never be removed or replaced, we conclude that there cannot be another covenant, in any proposed millennium, that will supercede or replace the gospel of Christ.

God kept His word. The New Covenant has been established by Christ through his death. There is not another covenant coming, and to suggest that there is, *especially another covenant that in every respect stands in opposition to the gospel*, is surely a dangerous thing to do.

The Dispensational Jeremiad Covenant would command virtually everything forbidden by the Gospel.

The proposed Dispensational Jeremiad Covenant forbids virtually everything that the Gospel mandates!

What happens to the Gospel therefore, in the Millennium?

So, What About *Israel* and the New Covenant?

The response to the above will be that the language of Jeremiah 31 is too specific to be ignored: the promise was that God would make the New Covenant with the house of Judah and the house of Israel. This demanded the "restoration of Israel" since the ten northern tribes were carried away captive by the Assyrians in the 8th century BC. They were "swallowed up by the Gentiles" (Hosea 8:8). So, the promise of a New Covenant with all twelve tribes would, of necessity, demand the restoration of Israel. This, we are told, simply has not happened, and will not happen until the Second Coming of Christ in fulfillment of Romans 11:25-27.

A full discussion of this issue would take us too far afield, take up too much space, so, I will only present a few "bullet points" that will hopefully promote more study on the part of the reader. The question is, did the NT writers believe that the promised restoration of Israel was taking place, that the New Covenant of Jeremiah was established– as the gospel? And the answer is yes. So, let's take a look at those bullet points and then, I will briefly develop each point.

✯ Virtually all of the writers of the NT were Jews steeped in Torah. This needs no documentation, so I will simply make the point.

✯ Those NT writers tell us that their eschatological hopes were nothing but the hope of Israel found in the Old Covenant promises made to Old Covenant Israel. For instance, the events of Pentecost were the fulfillment, actually the beginning of the fulfillment, of Joel 2, as Peter explicitly affirmed (Acts 2:15ff). Likewise, Peter said that the "restoration of all things" to be completed at Christ's second coming would fulfill God's promises to Israel found in Moses, Samuel and all the prophets, "all who have ever written" (Acts 3:21f). Paul said that his hope of the resurrection was grounded in "the law and the prophets" (Acts 24:14f).

✯ Those NT writers never, ever say that God's promises to Israel were being deferred, postponed or delayed.[16] They never, ever tell us that the church is a temporary measure, to be removed when the Lord turns again to Israel.[17]

✸ This point is critical: The NT writers, as suggested in the first point above, tell us that the OT promises that God made to Israel were being fulfilled in Christ and the church! Now, since we are focused on the subject of the New Covenant, let's investigate how that plays out in the NT.

Remember that the New Covenant was to be made with both houses of Israel. Consider carefully then the following reality that occurred on the day of Pentecost:

"And there were dwelling in Jerusalem Jews, devout men, from every nation under heaven. And when this sound occurred, the multitude came together, and were confused, because everyone heard them speak in his own language. Then they were all amazed and marveled, saying to one another, "Look, are not all these who speak Galileans? And how is it that we hear, each in our own language in which we were born? Parthians and Medes and Elamites, those dwelling in Mesopotamia, Judea and Cappadocia, Pontus and Asia, Phrygia and Pamphylia, Egypt and the parts of Libya adjoining Cyrene, visitors from Rome, both Jews and proselytes, Cretans and Arabs—we hear them speaking

---

[16] See my book *Seal Up Vision and Prophecy*, for a full discussion of the so-called Postponement doctrine. The idea that man could thwart or even delay God's unconditional promises is one of the saddest theological inventions of all time.

[17] See my book, *Leaving the Rapture Behind*, for a fuller discussion of this. (Ardmore, Ok. JaDon Management Inc., 2011). The book is available on my websites.

in our own tongues the wonderful works of God" (Acts 2:6-12).

So, on Pentecost, we have Hebrews / Israelites, from "every nation under heaven." It is not just Judahites, as some have tried to argue. The regions from which that audience came included, as we shall see, the regions of the "diaspora" to which the ten northern tribes were taken, according to Hosea.

There is an important point to be made here. The entire nation, every man, of all twelve tribes, did not have to be present for God to make the New Covenant with "the whole house of Israel." There was, in ancient Hebraic thought, the idea of representative actions.

When Israel was gathered at Sinai / Horeb, YHVH made the covenant with them. When He made the covenant with them that day, it was well understood that He was making the covenant for all of Israel in the generations to come (Deuteronomy 5). That generation represented the generations to come, in entering that covenant.

There was also the idea in Israel that one could make a covenant with representatives who represented the entire nation. When the Lord made the covenant of circumcision with Abraham, that covenant was applied to the entirety of Abraham's seed (Genesis 12:17f).

My point is that when Jesus shed his blood to confirm "the New Covenant" (Matthew 26:26f) and he made that covenant with the twelve apostles– he was signifying that he was making that covenant with the whole house of Israel. And then, when Peter stood up in front of that audience gathered from around the world, and he spoke to them of Christ, the Messiah, the one through whom the New Covenant was prophesied to come, he was sharing with them the promised New Covenant. There is not a word from Peter on that auspicious day that God's plans and promises had failed, or been postponed. Rather: "This that which was promised..."

☆ The OT promised that in the last days, God would make the New Covenant with Israel, when He "remarried" her. The NT writers tell us the betrothal had happened and the Wedding was at hand! This is where I have to be brief. For a fuller discussion see my *We Shall Meet Him In*

The Air.[18]

Here are a few critical points to guide us:

✔God was married to Israel (Isaiah 54:1f). That marriage took place at Sinai, in the giving of Torah (Jeremiah 31:29f).

✔The ten northern tribes broke that marriage covenant, becoming a "harlot wife" and as a result, God divorced her: "I am not her husband, and she is not my wife" (Hosea 2:1-3).

✔ God could not divorce Judah, even though she was equally unfaithful, because of the promise that He would bring Messiah through her (cf. Jeremiah 3:1-8). Nonetheless, YHVH said that the day was coming– in the time when He would save the remnant of all the people, that Judah would receive the same fate that the ten northern tribes had– national destruction (Hosea 6:7f).

✔ God promised that the day was coming when He would make the New Covenant with Israel, and: "I will betroth you to me in righteousness, I will betroth you to me for ever" (Hosea 2:18-19). This is where we must remember the first few points above: The New Testament writers had only one eschatological hope– the hope of Israel found in Torah. anticipated the fulfillment of God's promises to Israel. They never tell us that those promises were delayed, and, they tell us that those promises were being fulfilled in Christ and the church! Notice the following, ever so brief, few points:

☞ Paul said that he had betrothed the body of Christ to Christ, as a chaste virgin (2 Corinthians 11:1f). Now, if Paul preached nothing but the hope of Israel found in the OT, and if (since) Paul knew of the

---

[18] *We Shall Meet Him In The Air, The Wedding of the King of kings*, (Ardmore, Ok. JaDon Management Inc, 2011). The book is available on Amazon, Kindle, my websites and other retailers.

promise of the New Covenant remarriage of YHVH and Israel, then when he speaks of how the Corinthian church– part of the righteous remnant– had been betrothed to Christ, this is incredibly important! That betrothal cannot be "divorced" (pun intended) from Hosea's promise of the last days betrothal and remarriage– the New Covenant!

Consider again that Paul is addressing "Jews" (not *Judahites*) in Corinth. That city was outside of Palestine, the promised land; it was part of the Diaspora. So, for Paul to say the Corinthian saints, (those of the Diaspora synagogue who had now accepted Jesus as the promised New Covenant Messiah) had been betrothed to him, this is tantamount to saying that Hosea's promised New Covenant was being entered. But, the apostle Peter is even more explicit in affirming the fulfillment of God's promise of the last days fulfillment of Hosea's promise of the remarriage.

In 1 Peter, the apostle specifically says that he was addressing the Diaspora, the strangers scattered abroad:

"Peter, an apostle of Jesus Christ, "To the pilgrims of the Dispersion in Pontus, Galatia, Cappadocia, Asia, and Bithynia, elect according to the foreknowledge of God the Father, in sanctification of the Spirit, for obedience and sprinkling of the blood of Jesus Christ: Grace to you and peace be multiplied" (1 Peter 1:1-2).

Take note that the regions he addresses are some of the very regions represented on Pentecost.

✱ Peter calls them pilgrims of the Diaspora! This was a technical term for the ten tribes who had been dispersed.[19]

---

[19] It is extremely unfortunate that many commentators believe Peter was addressing the Gentiles, and not Diaspora Israelite Christians. This view completely misses the point that Peter is focused on the fulfillment of God's Old Covenant promises to restore the whole house of Israel, under Messiah and the New Covenant.

✱ Peter says he was living in the times foretold by the prophets and that he was interpreting the promises made by those Old Covenant promises, through the inspiration of the Spirit (1 Peter 1:10-12).

✱ Amazingly, Peter then cites, verbatim, the promise of Hosea concerning the restoration of Israel, under the New Covenant:

" But you are a chosen generation, a royal priesthood, a holy nation, His own special people, that you may proclaim the praises of Him who called you out of darkness into His marvelous light; who once were not a people but are now the people of God, who had not obtained mercy but now have obtained mercy" (1 Peter 2:9-11– citing Hosea 1:9f).

Here is the bottom line:

Hosea foretold the making of the New Covenant at the time of the restoration / remarriage between Israel and God.[20]

Peter wrote to the very ethnic people to whom those promises were made, the Diaspora, those scattered among the nations.

Peter said those promises were being fulfilled in Christ and the church– not in a nationalistic restoration of Israel to the physical land!

---

[20] It is highly significant that the promise of the New Covenant in Hosea 2:18 is couched in the language of the redemption of Creation! What this suggests is that Adamic Eschatology, to coin a term, would be overcome in the making of the New Covenant at the end of the Old Covenant! This establishes what I call *Torah to Telos*, i.e. the Biblical fact that the Law of Moses, Torah, would stand firm until the eschatological consummation. I cannot develop this here, but, see my argumentation along this line in my debate with Joel McDurmon, July 2012. The book of that debate, *End Times Dilemma*, is available from my websites, Amazon, Kindle and other retailers.

Notice Peter's interpretation of the OT promises– particularly of Hosea 3 - of the Messianic Temple in 1 Peter 2:4f. Peter makes it undeniably clear that through the Spirit it was being revealed that the promised Messianic Temple, established on Christ as the living corner stone, was *the spiritual body of Christ.* The promised priesthood was that of any believer in Christ, and the sacrifices were no longer the blood of bulls and goats offered on a physical altar! Everywhere we examine Peter's interpretation of those OT promises, he interpreted them spiritually- not literalistically.

What is so critical of course, is that Peter tells us that the Old Covenant prophets did not understand either the manner or the time when their prophecies would be fulfilled (1 Peter 1:10-12). But, he tells us that he was living in the anticipated time. Furthermore, he tells us that through the Spirit, he and the other apostles were revealing the true meaning of the things foretold, but not understood, by those OT prophets.

So, since Peter affirmed the first century fulfillment - in Christ - of God's Old Covenant promises to Old Covenant Israel– *promises that were concerned with the remarriage of Israel under the New Covenant -* then it is *prima facie* proof that the New Covenant was being made with "the whole house of Israel!"

The claim that God never made the New Covenant with both houses of Israel– or with Israel at all - is therefore falsified. In fact, consider this: with whom was the New Covenant made on Pentecost? It most assuredly was not with the Gentile nations! It was made with those "Jews, proselytes,[21] and "devout men, from every nation under heaven." To reiterate, that audience was comprised of Israelites. Not pagans, not Gentiles. And the fact that Peter affirmed repeatedly that the events of that day were the fulfillment of God's promises to Israel, found in

---

[21] This is hugely important. Under Torah, any pagan / Gentile, could become an "Israelite" to be considered as a "native born son" by joining himself to YHVH and through circumcision and baptism! *Blood did not matter!* See Exodus 12:48.

Torah, falsifies any idea that the kingdom promises had failed.

From Acts 2 until Acts 8, to whom was the gospel, (that Jesus called "the New Covenant") offered and preached? It was preached exclusively to Israel (to use the comprehensive term). In fact, from Acts 2-8 the Jewish Christians did not even go outside Jerusalem in preaching that New Covenant! Thus, once again, the claim that the church is the "Gentile" replacement of Israel has no merit for a period of literally years after Pentecost![22]

In Acts 8, following the outbreak of persecution against the church in Jerusalem, Philip went to Samaria.[23] This means he was not offering the church as a replacement for Israel, to the "Gentiles." No, he was preaching the restoration of Israel in Christ.[24]

And what did Philip preach? He did not preach delay. He did not proclaim "Replacement Theology" as is sometimes taught. He did not speak of Israel being temporarily set aside so that the Gentile church

---

[22] In fact, notice that in Acts 3:21f Peter makes a point of stating that the events unfolding in Jerusalem was the *fulfillment* of God's promises to Israel! He calls that Jewish audience's attention to the fact that God promised to bless "all the nations of the earth" through the Seed of Abraham, and that He had kept His promise in sending Jesus to Israel first. This can only mean that it was God's original intent to bless Israel first– which he said was happening– and then the nations. No postponement, no alteration of God's scheme.

[23] Do not fail to grasp that Samaria was part of the northern tribes, in spite of the fact that many of the original Israelites had been carried off. The historical fact is that many original members of the ten northern tribes remained in Samaria. Thus, the preaching of the kingdom / gospel in Samaria must be viewed as part of the restoration of Israel!

[24] See my "Acts and the Restoration of Israel" MP3 series. In this series I chronicle how Acts is indeed the story of the "re-formation" and the restoration of Israel, the New Creation in Christ. That series is available from my websites.

could stand until "the times of the Gentiles is fulfilled"[25] as most Premillennialists maintain. He preached the kingdom, just as Paul, even at the close of his ministry, said that he still proclaimed nothing but the hope of Israel and the kingdom (Acts 28:20, 23, 31).

Note the prominence of the outpouring and manifestation of the gifts of the Spirit in Acts 8, in the preaching of the Kingdom. It was a long held belief in Israel that the Holy Spirit and prophetic office had ceased in Israel. However, in the last days, and in the restoration of Israel, the Spirit would once again be poured out. That the Spirit was being given, in charismatic manifestation, powerfully communicated that the restoration of Israel was underway. The presence of the gifts of the Spirit meant the New Covenant was being delivered. This is not failure; this is fulfillment!

So, in Acts 8, it speaks of the preaching of the gospel, *which Jesus called the New Covenant*, in the regions of Samaria, i.e. Israel. The message was the message of the kingdom, confirmed by the outpouring of the Spirit, which was inextricably tied to the last days restoration / remarriage of Israel under Messiah and the New Covenant. How then is it possible for one to claim that what was being done in Samaria was unrelated to the establishment of the promised Jeremiad Covenant?

Skip forward now to 1 Peter once again. Remember the following points:

1. Peter was specifically addressing the Diaspora, the scattered tribes.

2. Peter tells his audience that through the (eschatological) Spirit he was interpreting the Old Covenant promises of the salvation to come at the parousia.

3. Peter then cites Old Covenant promises, including the prophecy of Hosea 3, of the restoration of the Temple, the priesthood, etc., and, he

---

[25] The Dispensational claim that the "Times of the Gentiles" refers to the period from Babylon, or from AD 70 until some time in the future when Israel is no longer dominated by the "Gentiles" is specious. See my YouTube debate (July 8, 2015) with Dr. Michael Brown.

unequivocally interprets those prophecies spiritually.

4. He then cites, verbatim, the prophecy of the restoration / remarriage of Israel (Hosea 1:9f) and says that it was being fulfilled in Christ (1 Peter 2:9ff).

Now, if Hosea's prophecy of the remarriage of Israel was being fulfilled in Christ, then the New Covenant promised by Hosea and Jeremiah was being fulfilled! And this being the case, the Dispensational claims that the Jeremiad Covenant has never been established are falsified.

The fact is that in 1 Peter, he was not, as so many commentators unfortunately claim, dealing with Gentile converts, calling them Israel, as a result of the "replacement" of Israel. He was addressing the same regions represented on the day of Pentecost, and he specifically used terminology that was considered a technical term for the scattered ten tribes! Peter was not positing a Gentile message per se- although he undeniably realized, per Acts 10 that the pagans were now included in the spiritual blessings of Christ. No, just like Philip he was preaching the restoration of Israel in fulfillment of God's promises to her.

Finally, back to Acts for a moment. Notice that Luke makes it a point to say this:

"Now those who were scattered after the persecution that arose over Stephen traveled as far as Phoenicia, Cyprus, and Antioch, preaching the word to no one but the Jews only. But some of them were men from Cyprus and Cyrene, who, when they had come to Antioch, spoke to the Hellenists, preaching the Lord Jesus" (Acts 11:19-20).

This retrospective look back at the time before Cornelius gives us insight into the composition of the early church for several years after Pentecost. *It was a Jewish church, and exclusively so!* There is simply no justification therefore, for the claim that the establishment of the church on Pentecost was the establishment of the "mystery" of the church– to replace Israel. For some ten years after Pentecost, there were not even any Gentiles in the church! How then, in the name of reason and truth, can it even be suggested that the church was a temporary "Gentile" replacement of Israel due to Israel's rejection of the kingdom?

The fact is that in the preaching of the gospel, the early record of Acts records tremendous success among the Jews: "And the hand of the Lord was with them, and a great number believed and turned to the Lord" (Acts 11:21).

So, in Acts, we find the proclamation of the gospel to "both houses of Israel" (Judah / Samaria) and in 1 Peter, we find the record of the preaching of the gospel to the Diaspora. More, we find the story of success, and the inspired commentary by the NT writers that what was happening through their preaching of the gospel was the fulfillment of Israel's promises. There is not one text that affirms, or suggests, the delay of the kingdom. Not one suggests that God's promises to Israel had been postponed or transferred away from them, and given to someone to whom they were never intended.[26] On the contrary, the calling of the Gentiles into Israel's salvation was always the plan (Isaiah 49:6f / 62 / 65-66).

The *original plan* was that God would make the New Covenant with the righteous remnant of all the house of Israel.

The *original plan* was that the Old Covenant and all vestiges therefore, be taken out of the way. This is why, as we noted above, it is so important to see the power of Hebrews 8:13 and the affirmation that when Hebrews was written, the Old Covenant was "nigh unto passing." This could only mean one thing: The New Covenant- of Jeremiah per Hebrews 8:6f - was about to fully take the place of the Old, just as promised!

The *original plan* was that the Gentiles would come into Israel's blessings. It is important to see that this is precisely what was taking place in the first century. See Romans 15:27.

---

[26] I cannot develop this but, it is critical to realize that it was always -*always* - God's plan that Old Covenant Israel would find the fulfillment of her promises in Christ and the church. Israel's rejection of those things justified the Lord in bringing judgment against that Old world, to bring in the promised New Creation. See my *Like Father Like Son, On Clouds of Glory*, for a fuller discussion of this important truth.

As we have seen in this work, the gospel of Christ gives and does everything promised by Jeremiah 31.

The New Covenant of Christ established through his blood, is far, far superior to the proposed Jeremiad Covenant of Dispensationalism.

The New Covenant of Christ forbids much of what the proposed Jeremiad Covenant supposedly will mandate. Thus, that proposed New Covenant cannot be the will of God. It is opposed to the gospel.

The Gospel of Christ will never fade away, never become obsolete, never be limited.

The Gospel of Christ is for all men, of all nations– including the Jews. There is not now, nor will there be a covenant for just the Jews. That would violate Paul's gospel decree that in Christ there is no Jew nor Greek. Thus, to be in Christ and the Gospel is to be saved. To be outside the Gospel, in any proposed Jeremiad Covenant exclusive of the Gospel, is to be outside Christ and salvation.

God is to be glorified, and man redeemed through the gospel, only the gospel, and not through any proposed additional and different future New Covenant that essentially makes a mockery of the gospel of Christ.

"Now to Him who is able to do exceedingly abundantly above all that we ask or think, according to the power that works in us, to Him be glory in the church by Christ Jesus to all generations, forever and ever. Amen!" (Ephesians 3:20-21).

Addendum: The Question of Two Covenants

We have noted the severe problem with the idea of there being two covenants in force in the Millennium. As noted, the Gospel forbids the very things that the proposed Jeremiad Covenant will supposedly mandate. So if, as Ice and other Dispensationalists propose, there will be only one covenant in force in the Millennium, then one covenant has to be jettisoned. That cannot be the unending Gospel of Christ!

The "alternative" - which Dispensationalists claim to eschew - is that there will be two covenants in effect in the Millennium. The Jeremiad Covenant for Israel and the Gospel for the Gentiles. The problem is, as we have noted, that this would mean that the Jews under the Jeremiad Covenant, will be commanded to do the very things that the Gospel condemns. Gentiles under the Gospel would be forbidden to do the things - keep the Sabbath and Feast days, etc. - that the Jeremiad Covenant not only commands, but condemns "the(Gentile) nations of the world," for not observing (Zechariah 14)! The idea of two disparate covenants, two totally *opposing* covenants, for two people is untenable.

About this time, opponents of Covenant Eschatology will claim that this is a self contradiction in the preterist viewpoint. After all, it is maintained by leading preterists that there were two covenants in effect for the forty years between the Cross and AD 70, Torah and the Gospel. So, if that could be true, the argument goes, why can there not be two covenants in effect at the same time in the Millennium. The objection fails on several points.

Let me note first of all that these opponents claim that God could never have two "laws" or systems in effect for different people at the same time. This is patently false, since it is indisputably true that God gave Torah to Israel, *but did not give it to the Gentiles* (Romans 2:14f). So, God most assuredly did deal with Jew and Gentile by two different means. But, the point to be grasped is that this was not His intended, permanent goal or plan.

Second, the two covenant state (Torah and Gospel) was not intended to be permanent or even beneficial. God did grant Israel a period of grace (Acts 3:19-24) to continue under Torah until the Gospel could be preached into all the world. *But, that Gospel proclamation was not a message to continue in the Old Covenant.*

Thirdly, and directly related, is the fact that during that interim grace period, those under Torah who accepted Christ "died to the law" in order to be married to Christ (Romans 6:4-7). In other words, they could not live in two worlds. The two worlds were definitely opposed to one another!

Fourth, and again, directly related, is the indisputable fact that the Gospel message to the Jews was that Torah was "nigh unto passing" (Hebrews 8:13) and that they were to come into the New Covenant. The Ministration of Death, written and engraven on stones, was passing away, giving way to the everlasting New Covenant Kingdom of Messiah (2 Corinthians 3 / Hebrews 12:25f). The Old Covenant, insufficient and weak, was typological of the better things of Christ and those better things were "about to come" (Hebrews 10:1-2) at the parousia of Christ.

While there is a great deal more that could be said about this issue, the point is that while there were two covenants existing side by side from the Cross to AD 70, that was not the "ideal." God did not "establish" that two covenant state as His ideal state, intended to bless those in the two covenants equally. The call - and the warning - to those under the law that commanded animal sacrifices, Festal observance, circumcision, etc. was that those things were shadows, they were insufficient and they were passing. The message was, the world of that Old Covenant was about to perish and they needed to come out and come into the one, eternal, life giving Gospel of the Messiah.

So, the fact that two covenants existed side by side for a short time in no way allows for two opposing covenants in the proposed Millennium. The forty year interim grace period was to bring the two covenant time to an end *because that was not God's ideal*. The end of the one covenant would fully establish the *one* eternal covenant. The Dispensational paradigm suggests that God really does want two opposing covenants to exist side by side. As we have seen, that is simply unbiblical and specious. As we have seen, the Gospel and the Gospel alone is God's eternal ideal.

Made in the USA
Middletown, DE
09 March 2020